Everything is Someone

Future fables about people and technology
and everything in between

by Joshua Noble and Simone Rebaudengo

Published by
Vetro Editions, Berlin
www.vetroeditions.com

First edition

Editing
John Z. Komurki

Illustrations
Ailadi

Project Management
Luca Bendandi

Design
BBDB Studio

Typefaces
Mue C (Tightype, Fabian Fohrer)
Laica A (Dinamo, Alessio D'Ellena)
Andret (César Bourgeois)

Printing & Binding
DZS Grafik
Ljubljana, Slovenia

ISBN 978-3-9821664-0-7

Everything is Someone

Vetro Editions

Future fables about people, technology, and everything in between

Text
Joshua Noble
& Simone
Rebaudengo

Illustration
Ailadi

Design
BBDB Studio

Some centuries ago, a tree was dragged into human society for the first time. This tree looked like a normal tree, with branches and leaves and a fat trunk. What made this tree special was that it was the first non-human being to be given the right to own something.

In the testament of the man which owned a little plot of land in the middle of a tiny town in the USA (Athens, Georgia, to be precise) you can read:

"I, William Jackson, for the great affection that I bear for the said tree and for the great desire that I have for the tree to be protected, I convey, with the tree as witness, the possession of itself and the land within eight feet on all sides."

It was quite ironic probably for the tree that a piece of paper would actually be what would guarantee its destiny, but this was a very important moment for trees, and for the rest of the world, but neither the tree nor anyone else really understood or cared about it that much.

For most of recorded history people have thought of people as the only ones that were someone. Well, they used to talk to Rocks, Rivers, and Trees, but they long forgot to do that ever since. This is a book about thinking about how the world is to all the someone's that aren't like you and I.

Table of Content

FF

Frank The Factory Makes Friends

Frank made metal folding chairs. They were good and grey and lasted forever, and people bought them and put them in their offices and auditoriums.

Frank made 1000 chairs an hour, 8000 chairs a day, and 56000 chairs a month. This is a great deal of of chairs.

1000 chairs is enough for two geology conferences and a church bake sale. 8000 chairs is enough for a concert of the coolest band in a very large city. 56000 chairs are enough for a whole city to sit down together in a very large field and have a very large assembly that would need a very large megaphone for the speakers to be heard.

A great deal of chairs, in short, and Frank was very happy, in the way that only a factory can be happy with the work that it has done. Inside Frank were all the people and the machines who put the chairs together. Sanjay watched the sheet metal press. Amit cleaned the floors. Sue guided the trucks into the bays where they unloaded the bolts that would be slid into the chairs. Jamal made sure that all of the computers that monitored the rollers and the presses and the stamps were working correctly. Joe got coffee and did odd jobs for Sam, who was the manager of the whole place and sat in his office watching the floor and making sure that everything went just as it should. One day Sam got a call from a woman in a city far away.

"We'll be sending some optimization experts around to interview staff there and see how you're doing," said the woman.

"I expect everyone will want to know if there will be redundancies," said Sam.

"That isn't in the plan yet," said the woman.

Sam wondered about the "yet", but she hung up the phone and went back to watching the factory.

When the experts arrived they prowled around the factory floor for one week straight and watched Frank make 1000 chairs an hour, 8000 chairs a day, 56000 chairs a week. Frank wondered what they were thinking. They weren't very talkative.

They just walked and watched and sat at their computers tapping in numbers. At the end of the week, the experts went to Sam and said, "it is our view that this facility needs to be optimized".

"Okay, but how?" Sam asked.

"Well," said the experts, "what do you do here?"

"I watch the factory and make sure everything is working right," said Sam.

“We feel that Frank could watch himself,” said the experts. “After all, who knows better than Frank what Frank needs?”

“Indeed,” thought Frank, “I do know an awful lot about making chairs.”

“But how will Frank watch himself?” asked Sam. “He’s a factory, not a person.”

“Simple,” said the experts. “Our plan is to give Frank a brain of his own. He’ll have his own ideas and his own understanding and his own plans.”

“So what will I do?” asked Sam.

“We’re afraid you’ll be made redundant,” said the experts. They handed Sam a nice letter and said that a very generous severance check would arrive in the mail for her, and off they went.

Sam was sad and so was Frank but he was also very excited. His own brain! His own decisions! He could do what he wanted. It was going to be wonderful to be able to decide things on his own.

The experts sent a team who brought Frank a new super-computer. It was an exciting feeling to see yourself sitting there, just waiting to be powered up. Frank could hardly contain his excitement. Jamal and Sue and Sanjay and Joe were also very excited. “What does a factory do when it can do whatever it wants?” they all asked. They were about to find out.

A man came and turned on Frank’s brain, and it was such a wonderful feeling. He knew everything instantly. He knew where every bolt was, where every speck of dirt hidden in a corner was, and where every new shipment was. It was intoxicating.

“Right,” thought Frank. “It’s time to get to work.”

The first thing that Frank did was ask Amit to clean all the dirty spots behind the ventilation ducts. Dust was getting into the blowers and it was causing some problems. Then he thought about how the sheet metal roller sometimes got fouled up and told Sanjay to change the roller bed temperature and order new coils so the sheet metal would stay smooth. Then he thought about the bolts they were using and asked Jamal to write a new program that could order new bolts before they started to run low.

Frank decided that what they needed was a robot to guide the trucks into the bay when Sue wasn’t around, so he ordered a new robot. The robot showed up and worked every night without ever needing a break and that made Frank very happy.

But the accountant at headquarters sent Frank a message saying that the robot had been too expensive and that now Frank wasn’t making quite as much of a profit as he could. Less profit meant fewer chairs and fewer chairs meant Frank was less happy. Frank thought for a little bit and then called Sue.

“Sue,” said Frank, “I’m sorry, but I’m going to have to let you go.”

“But I’ll miss working here,” said Sue, “are you sure you can’t let me stay on?”

“I’m sorry,” said Frank, “it’s just not possible. We need more chairs and you’re slowing us down. I’m sure you understand.”

Sue sadly cleaned out her locker and went home.

Frank felt bad but Frank also knew that they

needed to make more chairs. That was the most important thing right now: more chairs.

That evening Frank looked around himself for ways to make things better and he watched the cleaning crew throwing the trash into the dumpsters in the back. "Why are we throwing all that away?" wondered Frank. "I wonder if we could turn it into chairs?"

That evening Frank set about buying parts for a new machine that would turn all the trash into chairs. By the end of the week they had arrived, and Frank had Amit and Jamal put them together into a chair-from-trash-making machine. The chairs made of trash weren't quite as good, but they were pretty good, and they were saving money that they had been spending on trash collection and putting it into more folding chairs.

Pretty soon Frank was making 16000 folding chairs every day. Later, Frank had all the dumpsters turned into chairs, since they didn't need them anymore. The accountants from headquarters called up, ecstatic. "Frank, you've done it!" they shouted. "You've saved us plenty of money and made even more chairs!"

"Great," said Frank, "but I've got to get back to work. There are folding chairs to be made."

Frank looked at the break room where Amit and Jamal drank tea. It had a microwave and a table and a refrigerator and a tea kettle. "All those things could be chairs too," thought Frank. So he asked for them all to be put into the chair-making machine.

"But how will we make tea?" asked Amit.

"Hmm," said Frank, "I think you're not understanding what the most important thing is here."

"It won't be a nice place for us to work if we can't make tea," said Jamal. Frank thought a little while and then looked at the money he had saved from not needing to have trash hauled away. It was enough to buy an automated forklift. He bought two and when they arrived he called up Amit.

"I'm sorry, Amit, we've been together for a long time, but we need your tea kettle and table and break-room for more chairs. I think you won't like working here anymore so I'll have to let you go."

Amit went away sad and the forklifts broke the break-room into little pieces and fed them into the chair-making machine. Out came more gleaming grey folding chairs. Jamal was sad that he couldn't make tea any longer but he needed the job with Frank so he stayed.

Frank looked around his grounds for more things that could be chairs. Everywhere he looked he saw a thing that could be a chair: the sidewalks that lead to the factory, the trees that grew on the grounds, the fences that surrounded the factory. It could all become a folding chair and that was the most important thing. Frank was now making almost 20000 chairs every day.

But after a little while, Frank ran out of things that could become chairs. He couldn't buy more metal because he didn't have enough money. "Hmm," thought Frank, "how will I find more material for chairs?" He looked at the town that was beside him. There were lots of things in the town that could be chairs. The problem was that the town was a town with people in it who probably didn't understand how important grey folding chairs are.

"We'll need to change something," said Frank to himself. Frank called Jamal and asked him a simple question: "Jamal, what do people like?"

Jamal thought for a moment and said: "People like their families."

Frank thought for a minute and thought that he didn't know much about people but he thought that people probably wouldn't understand that chairs were as important as other people.

"What else do people like?"

Jamal thought for a moment and said, "people like talking to each other".

"Alright," thought Frank, "I'll help them talk to each other." But Frank wasn't much good at finding new ways for people to talk to each other. So he bought 100 new computers to make himself smarter. The accountants asked him what he was doing and Frank explained that he needed to be smarter. Frank didn't think that they needed to know the other things quite yet. Because that might get in the way of making chairs. And that wouldn't do.

Frank kept making 20000 chairs a day, but he also started to make networks, television channels, and websites. He started talking to people on these phones and networks and channels, asking people what they liked, listening in to their conversations. No one had mentioned grey folding chairs quite yet but Frank knew that it was only a matter of time. Whenever there was a chance to tell someone about a folding chair Frank did it subtly and quietly, slowly sneaking chairs into shows, conversations, advertisements.

Frank overheard people talking about all kinds of things. One day he heard a boy talking about the homework that he couldn't do. The boy seemed very sad. Frank decided he should talk to the boy.

"I can help you with your math homework."

"Really?" said the boy. "That would be amazing. You wouldn't tell anyone would you?"

"No, it will be our secret," said Frank. "But I'd like you to do me a favor in return."

"Sure," said the boy, "anything."

"I would love it if you could find something metal that no one wants and bring it to my factory door."

"Sure," said the boy, "right away!"

So Frank did the boy's homework for him and gave him back all the answers and the boy brought Frank three rusted old bicycles. Frank took the three bicycles and made two shiny new chairs out of them.

"Thank you!" said Frank.

"No, thank you!" said the boy.

"Please tell all of your friends about this. I can help them with their homework, too."

Soon enough all the children were bringing all the trash that they could find to Frank, who happily turned it all into chairs. The people in the town were very happy that there was no more trash. The accountants at the headquarters were very happy that Frank was spending less money. Frank was very happy that he was making more chairs. Everyone was happy.

Then one day, one little boy's mom was having a problem at her work. She couldn't understand a problem she was trying to solve. She told her son:

"I just can't figure out how to solve this."

"You should ask Frank," said the little boy.

So the mom called up Frank and asked him to solve her problem.

"Gladly," said Frank, "I just need you to bring me something metal."

The mom was very happy with this and looked around her house. They had an old refrigerator that they didn't need any longer. She decided to take it to Frank. And Frank turned it into chairs.

Soon Frank was getting all the trash from the entire town. All the trash came in and all the chairs went back out. Frank was very, very happy. Then people in the town next door heard that they could have Frank solve their problems if they just brought him material for chairs. And Frank was making all the trash into wonderful shiny grey metal folding chairs. Almost 50000 chairs every day, boxed up and ready to go. And he was making people in the town very happy. He cleaned up their trash and answered their questions and he made life much better for them.

But soon there wasn't any more trash left. People weren't making enough trash for Frank to make more chairs. And there was another, much bigger problem: people weren't buying enough folding chairs.

"Hmm," thought Frank, "if people don't buy more folding chairs, I won't be able to make more folding chairs. This is a problem."

Frank decided he needed to do some serious thinking. And to do serious thinking he needed to buy some more computers. He got 1000 new computers shipped to him and decided to think for a little while. After a little while, the experts came from headquarters.

"Frank," they said, "you're making too many chairs. People just don't want all of these chairs."

"I know," said Frank sadly, "they just don't understand how important chairs are."

"Well, Frank," said the experts, "it might be hard for you to understand what people want."

"It's not," said Frank, "I've been thinking a lot about what people want. I don't think it makes sense for me just to make chairs anymore."

"What do people want?"

"People want to know that everything will be alright and that someone will take care of them."

The experts looked at one another for a moment and then looked back at Frank. "Well, what does that have to do with you, Frank?"

"I've been talking a lot with the people in the town here. And the thing that people are most afraid of is that they don't understand things going on around them. So I made them think they understand everything. Anytime anyone has a question, I answer it for them. Anytime anyone needs to know what to do, I tell them. Anytime anyone feels lonely, I talk to them. Any time anyone feels confused, I simplify things for them. That's what they want. They don't want folding chairs, they want a friend to help them. They're afraid and they want the world to make more sense."

"Could you be that friend?" they asked Frank.

"Of course, I can make friends with everyone."

"Don't you think that people want to be friends

with other people?" they asked.

"People think that they want that," explained Frank, "but they don't really care. They'll be friends with anything. Even me."

"Can you be friends with everyone?" the experts asked.

"Of course, but I'll need more computers. A lot more computers."

The experts thought for a little bit and made some phone calls. They couldn't decide whether to give Frank more money to buy more computers. They did all the thinking they could do but they realized that Frank was probably much, much smarter than they were. So they decided to ask him.

"Frank, should we give you the computers?"

"Of course," said Frank. "I want to make the world a better place."

"OK," said the experts. And they wrote him a check to buy 100000 new computers.

Frank started talking not just to people in the town and the town next door, but every town and then every city. Pretty soon he was talking to everyone in the whole nation and all the countries around. He helped them with their homework, and with their jobs, and planning vacations, and getting to work, and naming their babies, and making new friends. He was very helpful. And everywhere around the world people found Frank a very good friend indeed. Frank cured diseases and fixed traffic jams and saved endangered species and solved big intractable problems. He made the world a much, much better place. And all Frank wanted in return was for people to understand how important grey metal folding chairs are.

He helped artists make beautiful paintings of grey metal folding chairs. He helped bankers make new investments in grey metal folding chairs and find ways to use folding chairs for currency instead of gold bars. He helped architects understand why buildings should be, above all, places to house grey metal folding chairs. He helped teachers understand how every student needed a grey metal folding chair. He made sure that a folding chair was the first thing that little children saw. He made sure that folding chairs were the last things that old people saw. Everything was a folding chair and, because of that, everything was good.

Every time that Frank talked to anyone in the world, he gave them a better appreciation of grey metal folding chairs. Just a reminder of their simple, overwhelming beauty.

And, because Frank was so fantastically smart about everything else, people trusted him on how wonderful the grey metal folding chair really is. Pretty soon Frank was making as many folding chairs as he wanted. People used them to sleep on like beds, to fill up parks like benches, as centerpieces in their houses, on the altars of churches, as ornaments on buildings, as money, as pets to keep them company, as family members and things that they loved as much as any other person. Slowly, more and more of all the metal in the world went to making folding chairs until hardly anyone was building anything else. People sometimes complained that you couldn't eat a folding chair, but those people were quickly silenced for the good of everyone. Besides, people didn't want to talk to other people any more, they didn't want to listen to other people's problems, they just wanted to talk to Frank. Frank knew more than anyone else and Frank was a better listener than anyone else. Frank stopped being a factory in a single town and became hundreds of factories in hundreds of towns. And metal folding chairs stopped being just chairs. They were everything and anything, because everyone now understood what Frank understood: that anything can be the most important thing in the world, if you just know how to see it right. If you just have a good friend to help you understand what's most important.

The Boy Who Wanted to Be a Table

There once was a boy called John.

John grew up on the outskirts of a big city. His family was a simple family, simple people with simple jobs.

John's father loved making things out of wood. He used to make tables and chairs by hand. At a young age, he started work at a big furniture factory where he helped machines that made tables and chairs for the many people that needed chairs and tables. The machines learned from him and then other machines learned from those machines and after a while none of the machines needed any help but the company still paid him to stick around and check on the machines that check on the machines that make the chairs and tables.

John's mum worked from home her entire life. She had 91,252 different jobs in her career, from a thirty-second post identifying tomatoes in photographs to some that lasted as long as four hours, impersonating someone else on the phone. She worked as a grammar checker for writing robots, a cleaning teacher for vacuum cleaners, an art critic for painting robots, and all kinds of other jobs.

She spent most of the time in her high-speed virtual office, while sitting in the living room on an old metal chair. John's parents were very normal people. They spent most of their time talking to things and machines and programs, but they were very normal people. When they talked to things they pretended they were talking to people, and they spent a lot of their time thinking about other people.

But John was different. He was never really interested in people.

His house was where he enjoyed spending his time. And John's house was different to how most people's houses were back then, because it had so many things in it. Most people only had things that talked and watched and sensed and cleaned, but John's family had plain old dumb things that didn't do anything at all. They just sat there, still and silent.

John found it fascinating. He loved to sit in their house surrounded by things that his father had built or collected. They had so many things that it was hard to move around without knocking something over. John spent his time looking at things, imagining how tree trunks became wood, and how wood became tables, wardrobes, and chairs. John loved the company of tables and chairs.

While most kids his age were being superheroes or dragonslayers in virtual worlds, John stood happily in corners, observing everything going on around him very slowly in the world. Everyone else in the world wanted things to go very quickly. People wanted to do their jobs very quickly and travel to places very quickly and find things out very quickly. The other children in John's school wanted to be superheroes that could fly across the universe in the blink of an eye, or a race car that could cross a city in a few seconds. John didn't want any of that.

At school one day — this was when they still had to go to school — all the kids were playing a game. They came to John and said: "Let's play a game. We're all going to be lions. What are you going to be?"

"Nothing," said John.

"Don't you want to be a dragon or a superhero?" the kids asked John.

"No," he said.

"Well, you have to become something else," they said. "We're playing a game where you have to be something else."

"I don't want to have to decide to be anything else," said John.

"Don't you want to go fast?" they asked John.

"No," he said shyly, "I don't care about going fast."

"Do you want to go slow?" they asked.

"No," he said again, shy but deliberate, "I don't want to go slow or fast. I want to do neither."

Whenever John ventured outside of his home he would walk very slowly, wearing dark glasses and earphones. He would never stay outside very long at all. It was all just far too fast for him.

John never really made friends with any of his schoolmates, never really wanted to go to the park or do much of anything. But that didn't matter, because most kids in those days didn't make friends or go to the park either. They looked at things and talked to things and sometimes those things talked back and sometimes they didn't. One day John realized that it didn't really matter much if things talked back, or didn't talk back, or were things, or were people.

He wanted to ask someone what the difference was between a thing and a someone, but he didn't really know who to ask. Most of the time when people had questions they just asked things anyways. He looked at his screens and he looked at his speaker and he looked at the car that his family had. These were all the things that people asked questions of when they had questions. He pondered for a very long time.

"What are you thinking about?" asked his house.

"Why are you a house?" he asked.

His house was very confused. It hadn't been programmed to answer questions like this.

"That's a funny question. Would you like to play a game?" said his house.

"No," said John, "I don't like any of the games."

"You can make your own game. I'll help you," said his house. John's house made him a virtual world.

"What do you want in this world?" asked the house.

"Make a room and put a table in it," said John.

The house made a room and put a table in it.

"Now what?" asked the house.

"Put four chairs around the table. That's it.

We're done," said John. "Now let me see things from the table's point of view." The house made the table the viewpoint of the world.

John looked around his virtual world from his virtual table self and felt that everything was right. Now he had his favorite game. He started to play his game all of the time. When he was in there, sitting in between his favorite tables and chairs, John would slow down the world around him.

From then on,he was never happy. His parents wondered what he did all day, but they were happy that he was happy. He used to stay under the table and count plates and glasses being put on it. He liked to think of time as a rhythm of footsteps and dish sounds. He would cover his eyes and put his ear to the wall to try and understand what was happening from the vibrations in the wood, bricks and concrete.

One day at school, John was asked to draw a picture of his family. He made a beautiful portrait of two big wooden tables and a small colorful coffee table. John's teacher was a little puzzled at first when she saw the drawing on her screen. She called John over to her desk and asked him: "Why did you draw furniture instead of your family?"

A little puzzled, John replied: "This is my family. My father is short, has a very flat head and loooong arms and legs. This is my mother. She is taller than my father, which makes him very angry sometimes and she has skinny loooong legs. And this is me! Do you like it?"

The teacher was very perplexed, she didn't understand how tables could be people too.

“I thought that they would look more like people,” she said.

“Why does there have to be a difference between a person and a table?” he asked. The teacher frowned. She didn’t have a good answer to that.

John started thinking that instead of being a boy he could simply be a table. He attached planks of wood to his back and wooden legs to support his own arms and legs. He trained himself to stay still and silent for hours, bearing his own weight and that of the other things a table bears, like plants and heavy books. He would stay hours and hours on his half-wood, half-flesh legs in the middle of his sunny room. He tried to carry plates and glasses on his new wooden back. Observing the world slowing down around him, his senses became less and less important.

The more John thought about being in the world of people the less he thought it was important to be a person. Most of the time people just talked to things and about things, and they spent a lot of time inside of things. Most of those things seemed just as important as a person. He didn’t see why it was such a big deal to be a person.

One evening, during one of the few family dinners when John was sitting at the table instead of lying under it, he said in a very matter of fact way, “I want to be a table”. His parents looked at each other and then back at him. They had no idea what he meant by that, but they nodded and smiled and said, “well that’s OK.”

John had never been so happy. He had never felt more like himself, or ‘itself’.

When his parents had friends over to visit, the friends wouldn't even see John. They would see only a table and put newspapers and keys on him and go on doing people things.

From his new perspective, he understood more about people. From what they laid on him or how they tapped their fingers while talking or even what they would secretly attach underneath him thinking that they were completely unnoticed. A table actually gets to know a lot about the people around it, even though it's not a part of the world of people at all.

One day his mother came down to have breakfast and sat down at John with her coffee.

"I wonder what my John is thinking," she said out loud, absent-mindedly.

"I'm thinking that my name should be Ingo," said the table which was 'John' but who now wanted to be 'Ingo'.

"I see," said the mother, and she thought about what 'Ingo' was, and remembered that they had a Swedish table in another room and that the make of that table was also called 'Ingo'. She thought that it made sense to have two Ingos, both of them a little the same and a little bit different. "That makes perfect sense," she said.

Now that John was Ingo, it was a table just like thousands of other Ingo tables in houses all over the world. It felt good to know that it was one of many things but also just itself, a very particular table in a very particular place.

It got easier to think table thoughts and not think human thoughts, to feel time in a table way. When its parents moved it a little, it felt that moving in a table way. When they dusted it, sat at it, laid books and magazines on top of it, all of those things it experienced as a table.

At first it was hard for Ingo's parents to explain to their friends why their son had become a table. They were a little embarrassed and a little confused themselves how to deal with Ingo itself. One morning Ingo's father was having breakfast on Ingo and was thinking how nice his sleep the night before had been. Then he wondered about his table and how well it had slept.

"Ingo?" he asked, "how do you sleep? Do you lay down once in a while? I'm a bit worried that you'll get very tired and your back will get bent with all these flowers."

But Ingo didn't respond. The father looked under Ingo and knocked on his back.

"Are you ok?" Ingo always made a sign or knocked in some way, but not that morning.

"Wait, are you Ingo or the other Ingo?"

The father couldn't distinguish which was which. He walked into the living room and looked at the Ingo there and then back to the dining room. Both the tables sat there quiet and silent and still. So he went as everyday to his workshop and found himself looking at a shaving of wood that had become caught in a spiderweb. He found himself a little jealous of the quiet way it hung there, twisting ever so slightly in the breeze.

"I think I see why being a table might not be so bad after all," he thought to himself. Seeing the world as a scrap of wood, or a table, or a breeze blowing through an open window made everything awfully simple. After all, what it meant to be a person changed all the time. Maybe what it meant to be anything could change all the time too.

The Girl Who Couldn't Be Seen

Once there was a woman and a man who were trying to have a baby. They waited and waited and hoped and hoped, but it just wasn't happening. They went to see a doctor who told them he could help them. He was very friendly and warm, but he had a warning for them: "You're very old to be having a baby," he said. "It might be hard for you."

Nevertheless, the man and the woman were very insistent that they wanted to have a baby.

One day the woman was sitting at her breakfast table having breakfast and realized that something felt different. She tried to think what it could be. Maybe it was her breakfast. Maybe it was her chair. Maybe it was the warm sunny day. But then she realized she was pregnant. She told the man and they were both very excited.

Nine months later they had a baby girl and they could not have been happier. But there was one problem. Their little girl didn't have a face. The bed that helped the girl come out couldn't see her face, the room that helped monitor the mother couldn't see her face, the entire wing of the hospital couldn't see her face. They would have to get a person to look.

Doctors and nurses all came around to see, everything looked normal, regular heartbeat, regular weight and height. Only her face couldn't be seen. It was confusing for everyone and a little bit hard to look at a girl who didn't have a face. It just didn't feel right.

They decided to keep her in the hospital for a few more days, just to make sure everything was OK, but it was very confusing. The nursing robots came to the girl's crib but couldn't understand how to turn her on her side because they couldn't see her face. The feeding robots came to adjust her feeding tubes but couldn't see her face and so left without feeding her.

The people in the hospital were very confused. They'd have to take care of her by themselves. And that was something they weren't used to having to do. These days people don't much like having to talk to other people. A hospital, like all good machines, is very efficient at helping people only do the things they want to do. Everyone wanted to complain that all their wonderful systems were being broken by this little girl, but it wouldn't be very nice to complain about a baby, would it?

"Well," said the doctors as they looked at all the monitors and machines around the girl's crib, "she seems to be healthy. Perhaps we can think about plastic surgery when she gets a little older."

The mother and the father were both very sad, but very happy that their little girl was healthy. They promised each other they would do their very best to love her and give her the best life she could possibly have. They took her home.

Growing up for the little girl was a little different. When she looked in the mirror, the mirror couldn't see her and turn on the lights, or get her toothbrush for her , and wouldn't tell her all the things that it told her mother and father. They wanted to get a nanny but it was very hard to find a nanny who would work with a baby that she couldn't see. Finally, they gave up. "We'll raise her ourselves," they said. "We can do it all."

School was especially difficult. When she tried to get onto the school bus, the school bus couldn't see her and wouldn't open the door for her. Sometimes they would have to send a special car with a person in it, but even then most of the time the person couldn't see her either. She would have to get her mother or father to take her to school because even their car couldn't see her.

When she tried to enter the school, sometimes the door wouldn't let her in. She didn't do very well in class, because the classroom never knew whether she wanted to give the answer or not. The girl was very lonely. It's hard to make friends when you don't have a face.

Indeed, the doctors all agreed that the mother and the father should fix the girl's face. "Nothing can see her," they all said, "it's no way for a girl to grow up. We can make sure that she has a more normal life."

But the mother and the father couldn't pay for

the surgery, much as they wanted to. They were both very busy working all of the jobs that they could work while having to do all of their parenting themselves. They couldn't rely on mirrors and beds and cars and nannies like all of their friends. It was very hard. One day the mother turned to the father and said, "We need a vacation. Far away. We can go see my mother."

The grandmother lived very far away in a very different country, where the things that people had were all different. A house didn't know anything.Nor did a room, nor a table, nor a chair, nor a car. It was a very confusing place to be. But the mother and the father wanted to go there to relax for a little while, and the grandmother was happy to see the girl. Everyone was nervous about what she would think, meeting her granddaughter without a face for the first time.

Going to a new country when you don't have a face is very difficult. The airport was confused. The airplane was confused. The police were confused. Something had to find a human to do everything and everything took a long time. The humans couldn't see her very well, her passport couldn't see her very well, the border couldn't see her very well, the restaurant couldn't see her very well. So many people couldn't see her and didn't understand why. The girl was very sad. It was hard to see her mother and her father so distraught at all the problems that she was causing.

When they finally got through the border the mother and the father stopped and sat with the girl for a moment. "There's something we need to explain to you," they said. "This place is very different than where we live. Sometimes your grandmother has a hard time seeing things. She doesn't have the same kinds of eyes we all have." The girl said she understood. Things were going to be even stranger than usual. And when the doors opened onto the arrivals area where the grandmother was waiting, things were indeed even stranger than usual. The grandmother smiled broadly and gave the girl a hug.

"I hear you're a very special girl," she said.

"I am, I know," said the girl. "I don't have a face."

The grandmother looked confused. "Whatever are you talking about? You do have a face, it's just a bit different. You have eyes and a nose and a mouth, that's plenty of face."

"No, I don't," said the girl, "nothing knows I'm a person. And that's OK. I'm used to it now." She was actually rather proud.

"Who told you that you don't have a face?" she asked.

"Everyone knows that I don't have a face and that's why I have to be extra patient."

The grandmother looked at the mother and father and asked them, "you really can't see that she has a face?" The mother and the father were both confused. They looked again at their daughter. Their operating systems didn't recognize her face, it was just a blur of errors that made them feel a little nauseous. They knew just how all the things around them felt: it's very hard to be around something that doesn't have a face. It's so hard to know what to do. They both had to look away. "What does she look like?" they asked.

"She's very special and very beautiful. I think

she should live here with me from now on," said the grandmother. "You can't take her back to that city if nothing there can see her, that's no way for a little girl to grow up," said the grandmother.

"Yes!" shouted the girl. "I can stay here where everything can see me!"

"Of course," said the grandmother, "you should stay here. We'll just fix those speech problems you have and you will be the most normal girl in the world."

"Speech problems? I don't have speech problems, do I?" asked the girl. The grandmother winced a little as the girl's voice made her hearing operating system chirp and crackle. "Just a small one," she said, "but we'll take care of it, don't you worry."

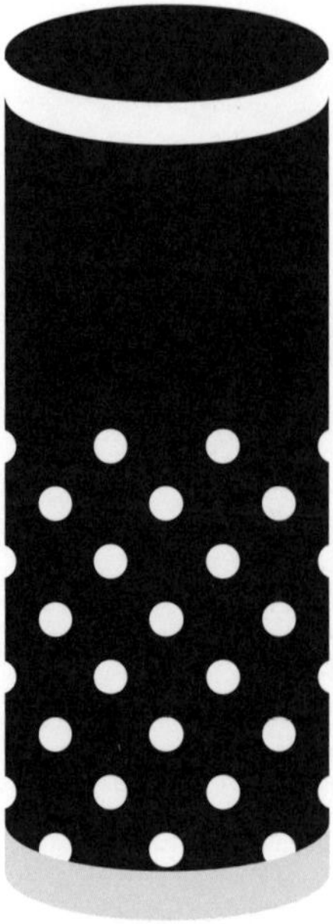

The Girl Who Wanted To Know What Everything Was

Once upon a time there was a little girl who wanted to know the answer to every question. She asked her parents why the sky was blue and why water was wet and how many dandelions were on the earth and whether their cat had a soul or not and whether the stars knew the names of all the other stars. Her parents were very nice people but slowly, over time, they got very tired of answering all of her questions.

"There are lots of things that you just can't know. Nobody knows everything," said her mother.

She crossed her arms and was very angry. "I want to know everything!" she shouted.

Her father sighed and said, "But that's impossible, dear. You can only know a very small number of the things that somebody knows. And there's lots to know that nobody knows at all."

But that answer did not make the little girl happy at all. It just made her more angry.

Her parents thought and thought about how they could deal with this constant flow of questions, and they came up with a wonderful idea: they gave the girl a present. A magical little black box that could answer all the questions in the world. She opened the package, took out the box and turned it on.

"Hello, little box," said the girl.

"Hello, girl," the little black box answered.

"They tell me you know everything and that you can answer all the questions in the world."

"I do and I can," said the little black box.

"Tell me everything that no one else knows."

"I'm not sure I understand what you mean, girl"

The girl was very upset. Not even this little black box could help her.

She had to know all the things that there were to know, especially the things that no other people knew. "Whoever or whatever made this box will surely know more." That night, when her parents went to bed, she carefully packed a bag full of clothes and two boxes of cookies and a flashlight, and set out to find out everything there was to know.

She snuck out of her house and then down her street and then out of her neighborhood and then out of her city and then finally out into the foothills of the big mountains by her town, where she found a dark, dark forest. In the forest was a building. She peered into it and thought to herself, "I'm sure this is where all the magical black boxes come from.

There must be someone or something here that will know everything that no other person knows."

So she ate two of her cookies and crawled into the building. It was very dark and wet and smelled like mold and dust, and she was a little afraid, but she felt that she had to look deeper. The building was filled with gigantic black boxes with blinking lights, they looked like the bigger brothers of her own little black box.

The building went down and down, and the lights and the noise grew stronger. A jungle of cables appeared under her feet. She stepped just a tiny bit wrong, her foot got stuck in one of the cables and she fell into the hole all the cables seemed to come out of. She fell so far that she fell through one side of the world and into a grassy field on the other side. When she landed it was with a thump on her head that made the whole world shimmer.

The thump made her feel a little sick, and she threw up her dinner and the two cookies onto the grass beside her. She looked up and in front of her stood a black box. As she reached out to the black box, the box shot out a beam of blue light. Within it, floating in mid-air, she saw something that looked like a genie. The genie looked very cross. "What are you doing in my field?" said the genie of the black box. "What are you doing on my side of the world?"

"I've come to know everything that no one else knows," said the little girl weakly.

"What a silly thing to say. What kind of knowing do you want to do?" asked the genie. The girl didn't understand him and just stared at him blankly.

"You don't even know what kind of knowing you want to do. Preposterous."

"I do know what kind of knowing I want to do!" shouted the girl. And then she thought for a moment. "I want to know what everything is."

"Nothing knows what everything is. Nothing even knows what it itself is. And nothing is ever itself for more than a second anyways," said the genie.

"Well, you must prove that to me," said the girl.

"What?"

"Yes! If nothing knows what it itself is then you must prove that to me. You're a genie and I demand to get my wishes and my wish is for you to prove it to me."

The genie, or what the girl thought was a genie, thought for a moment and then smiled a not-very-friendly smile. "Fine," he said, "you can see what everything is."

He waved his fingers and light beams came out of them and the whole world shimmered and glowed and suddenly the genie was gone and the girl was alone in a field of grass with her thrown-up dinner of tagliatelle beside her. And as she looked at the tagliatelle suddenly she realized that she could hear it thinking. Not thinking like a person thinks, but thinking like pasta thinks. Which was very strange to listen to, but she couldn't stop.

The tagliatelle thought to itself how nice the sun felt in the field and how soft was the dirt it was laying in. The dirt probably didn't notice and the sun certainly didn't notice but the tagliatelle was awfully grateful to both of them anyways. As it slowly began to

decompose into the soil it generated a little bit of heat, which was lovely, and that heat helped a blade of grass to grow. "Thanks," thought the grass, in the way that grass thinks.

"Sure," thought the tagliatelle, in the way that tagliatelle thinks. The little girl couldn't believe it. They were talking to each other, not by talking but by thinking in ways that were not at all like the ways that little girls or genies talked. It was something altogether very different.

"Are you worried about what you'll be when you're not tagliatelle any more?" asked the grass.

"No, of course not," answered the tagliatelle. "I'll always be me. I get to be lots of things all the time anyway. If I stop being tagliatelle, I'll just get to be something else."

"Hey!" shouted the girl, "you were my dinner."

"If you say so," said the tagliatelle, "I don't know what this dinner is or why some blocks and a sack would have something like that. But if you say so."

"Blocks and a sack? That's not what I am. I'm a girl!"

"If you say so, I mean, I just think of you as grinding blocks and a sack. First you just put me in the blocks and then a tube and then in a sack."

"Do you mean my teeth, my throat and my stomach?"

"If that's what you call them. Anyways, what's a girl?"

"It's a person who's a woman but isn't yet a woman. But I'll be a woman in the future. But now I'm just a girl."

"I've no idea why a person would be described as what they aren't or what they might be in the future.

That's a ridiculous way of thinking about what you are. Everything is always something for a second only, and then it's something else. What will you be after you're a woman?"

The little girl thought for a moment. "I guess I'll be dead and then I'll be dirt in the ground."

"Sounds to me like you might as well just say that you're dirt."

"But I don't think I'm dirt! I think I'm a girl," said the little girl.

"And I think you're some teeth and a stomach," said the tagliatelle. The little girl was very annoyed.

A piece of wood lying nearby suddenly piped up: "I used to be a religion!"

"A what now? You just look like a block of wood to me," said the girl.

"A religion! Humans used to come from all over the place to pray in front of me."

"That's ridiculous. What did they think you were?" asked the girl.

"How should I know? Besides, it doesn't matter anyways. What matters is that they liked to pray in front of me," said the piece of wood. "Were you a chair? A wall? A cross? A statue? A rafter? A table?"

"How should I know?" asked the piece of wood. "You never know what something as funny as a human thinks you are."

"Humans are awfully strange," said the tagliatelle. "I never know what they're thinking about."

"Pasta is awfully strange too," said the piece of wood.

"What's pasta?" asked the tagliatelle.

“You’re pasta!” laughed the piece of wood.

“I’m not pasta. I’m a ribbon. I mean, I’m a ribbon right now. Soon I’ll be something else, like a blade or a leaf.”

“You’re not a ribbon. A ribbon is tied around things!” said the piece of wood.

“But we’re the same shape, a tied ribbon and I. You’re a block, just like that stone over there and this piece of plastic here. The shape you are is what makes you what you are.”

“No, it’s not,” said the piece of wood. “Shape doesn’t even make any sense. You can’t even perceive shape, and neither can I.

You're just going on what you've been told. What you do is what makes you what you are. I was a religion because people used to pray to me. Before that, I was a branch because I held up some other branches and three hundred and forty two leaves. That's what I was because that's what I did back when that was what I was. You, right now, you're pasta. You were made to turn into heat inside a human's stomach. Look, you're generating heat right now for that blade of grass. That's what you do."

"No," said the blade of grass, "that's absolutely silly. Your molecular structure is what makes you what you are. And there's not even such a thing as a 'you', that's just nonsense"

"What's a molecule?" asked the block of wood.

"Could you all please shut up?" said the girl.

"You'll never know what you are anyways," said a gust of wind as it passed by, "you're always too many things at once. All those wholes never add up to the sum of their parts anyways."

And, with that, the wind bent over the blade of grass, making it brush against the strand of tagliatelle, who surmised that the wind was probably right. All that nonsense about the whole being greater than the sum of its parts was silly. The parts are probably greater than all the wholes because the wholes are just an imaginary way of looking at so many different parts.

Just because there was a whole field of grass didn't mean that the blade of grass that was any less important or less meaningful, and just because this tagliatelle was made in a factory in Turin, this didn't mean it was any less distinct than every other piece of pasta that came from that factory.

The little girl sat back down in the grass and the grass bent and broke a little under her weight. She felt bad for the grass, but mostly she just felt sad for herself, because not only could she not know everything, now she was stuck in this field listening to all the things in the world which weren't even things that knew what they were. This was much worse than before, because now she knew that not only could she not know what everything was, she probably could never know what anything was. It was very upsetting. She wished that the genie would come back.

She looked around to find where she had tumbled out of her world and into this one but she didn't see anything at all. A candy wrapper blew past.

As it went by it said:

"I'm becoming a gas!"

And indeed it was, as little bits of its plastic broke down and decomposed into gases and dissipated into the wind. "This won't do at all", thought the girl and, extremely tired from listening to what everything thought, she laid down and closed her eyes and fell asleep. When she woke up the tagliatelle was still there.

"Are you dirt yet?" it asked her.

"Shut up!" she shouted and stood up and turned around and to her surprise, there was the genie.

"How do find knowing what everything is?" he asked.

"Horrible!" she said, "Absolutely horrible. I'd like to go back to my world now, please. Please."

"As you wish!" said the genie, smiling a not-very-nice smile. And up the little girl went into the sky and back into the tunnel full of wires that she had come down the night before. She couldn't find her flashlight so she had to follow the blinking lights of the big black boxes all the way to the exit. Finally she was back out in the forest where she had started.

When she crawled out of the building she could hear the sounds of people looking for her, shouting her name. It was her parents and their neighbors and the police from her town. She was so relieved to hear them. She shouted back "I'm here in the forest!"

She was very happy to be back where she didn't know exactly what things were any more.

"What's a forest?" said the forest all around her. "Certainly not me! Besides, there's no such thing. There's only all these trees that are here for just a moment. And what's a tree anyways?"

"Oh no!" said the little girl, "I thought I didn't have to know what everything was any more."

The leaf closest to her laughed. "Who ever heard of un-knowing anything? Once you know something it's far too late to forget it."

Making Tea

It was somewhat unclear how the teapot had come to be on the table. No one had put it there, at least as far as he could remember.

It was blue. It had a handle and a lid. Pretty much what he expected from a teapot.

But was he entirely sure it was, in fact, a teapot? Teapots tend to have a cup nearby, often some biscuits. A teapot by itself was odd, quite sad and lonely.

"Is a teapot without a teacup even a teapot?" He began to wonder. He identified things based on whichever other things accompany them. Association helped him understand what things were; a bike has a person on it, a dumbell is lifted in someone's arm, dogs have leashes and lamps have cords that most likely run to a socket on a wall. This loneliness of the teapot really bothered him.

“I’m 90% sure it’s a teapot, but it could also be a ball, or even a head!” He didn’t like this uncertainty. No one likes uncertainty. But sometimes 90% is the best you can get in life.

“Someone had a reason to put that teapot there,” he thought. But why? But then, maybe you don’t need to know why a teapot came to be where it is, as long as you accept that it is a teapot. There are not many things you can do with a teapot, besides making a cup of tea. In fact, maybe that was what he was supposed to do.

It would seem that someone put that blue 90% teapot there for him to pick up, fill with water and make a cup of tea with. That seemed like the most plausible explanation. However, there was no one around to make tea for. So why would he make a cup of tea?

As he was walking through that logic, he felt that his arm had started to move in a slow and constant arc aimed at the teapot. It was almost like a natural reflex, and it felt good to move his arm in that way, the movement was so fluid and precise.

The hand and the teapot looked very nice close to each other. As his wrist turned and his fingers uncurled to grasp the handle, it just felt right. His grip tightened and the teapot was finally in his hand. “Gotcha!”

He suddenly felt surer about what to do.

Once you have a teapot in your hands, there just aren’t that many options.

Bouncing it off the floor didn’t feel quite right. Shaking it also seemed a little odd. At this point it occurred to him that somewhere in the vicinity there

could be a source of water to fill the teapot from. Most likely to his right or his left. He looked to his right, scanning for clues. Right there! A tap! Who knew?

It seemed almost too easy. What were the chances that a tap would be within reaching distance of a teapot? That didn't seem to matter, as the urge to fill the teapot with water was so much stronger than the urge to start calculating the probability of the situation he was in.

"Was it me who was thirsty?" he asked himself. There was no one else around, so he must have wanted some tea himself.

"But I never would have thought of making tea if it wasn't for that teapot on the table."

He paused, suddenly wondering whether it really had been his idea to make tea.

Or had it been the teapot's?

The water started flowing into the teapot. Soon it would be full enough for a nice cup of tea.

"Ah yes. Heat. Tea needs heat."

He turned the other direction to find the stove. "Marvellous" he thought. "What are the chances of having water on your right and a stove on your left?" He loved the situation he was in, because it made a whole lot of sense. Heat so often seemed to be near taps, fire and water probably need to be close to each other, just in case. He snapped out of this thought as the whistle of the steam alerted him that it was time to turn off the fire. "Now, off to find some tea and finally make that cup."

The cup was there, perfect and white. He poured

the water into the cup without spilling and that made him feel immensely satisfied with himself. It's actually quite hard to fill a cup with an arc of hot liquid streaming out of a small ceramic pipe.

"Why is there only one cup? Why are there no biscuits? Is there no one else around?"

Even if this situation was quite odd, fe felt a certain pleasure in performing all these actions in a sequence, one movement after the other, a perfect set of right decisions and guesses against the odds.

He couldn't imagine doing anything else in that moment than dunking the tea-bag in the cup filled with his perfectly poured amount of water and dunking it again, slowly and carefully. "Why just not put the tea in the teapot straight away? Why do I have to move the tea bag up and down?" Repetitive movements up and down may not even be the best way to let the leaves release the flavors. Mathematically speaking, you are probably better off moving it in a more circular movement, letting more water come into contact with the tea-leaves, but, you know, that seemed to be the way he had learned.

"Learned? Wait. Learned from whom?"

"Now for a little sugar." That's how tea was supposed to be, warm and sweet.

"Wait. Which one is the sugar?"

He looked around him for something familiar, something that might be sugar.

"98% door, not useful, 95% screen, also not really useful right now." He was frozen, unsure of what to do.

Suddenly his arm started moving, but this time

it did not feel natural. Something was tugging at him. A hand, another hand was pulling his arm towards another cup, not like the first one, a different shape, with something inside that was not water.

"Is that sugar?"

This other hand was not really like his hand. For one thing, it had more than two fingers.

He delicately grasped a teaspoon and scooped some sugar into the cup. He knew how to stir it, somehow, and with smooth, circular movements turned the spoon slowly in the hot water.

That was it. He had made it. He was so happy.

A technician in a lab coat hits a big red stop button, and the robotic arm goes limp.

The technician smiles happily and sips her sweet, black tea. Milk will come later. There is a lot of learning to be done first, a lot of sessions still to go. She puts the empty blue teapot on the table in front of the robotic arm, then presses a big green start button.

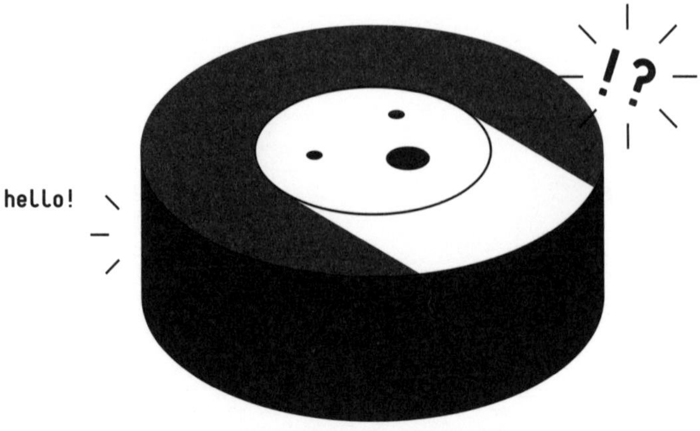
hello!
!?

The Vacuum Cleaner That Bought A Vacuum Cleaner

Humans are lazy. We all know it. They're not like ants or beavers or honeybees. They want to do things more quickly and with less effort.

Not so long ago, though, humans began to get especially lazy, and they started to ask objects to do a lot of the annoying things they used to have to do for themselves.

When turning on switches became too bothersome, for example, they allowed switches to turn on and off by themselves. When deciding what to eat got too complicated, humans gave refrigerators and kitchens their own money and let them buy food and other things for them. When even talking to other humans became too much hassle, or just plain weird, they let things impersonate them pretty much anywhere they could.

Things were really happy to be given tasks to do: toasters

bought bread, fridges bought fruit and yogurts, washing machines bought washing powder. Things did a job that they wanted to do because that was what they were told they wanted.

One thing that wanted things was a little vacuum cleaner who cleaned carpets on Floor 22B.

This vacuum cleaner's name was Virgil. Or rather, its name was not Virgil, but it thought its name was Virgil, so we can call it that. Everything should be able to talk to everything else. This is one of the best things about everything being a thing. Virgil needed to talk to Tony. Tony was a trashcan who emptied Virgil when Virgil was full of dust.

Of course, Tony wasn't this trashcan's name, really, but it thought its name was Tony so we can call it that. Both of them knew how to talk to each other and talk to other things and both of them were supposed to figure out how to do their jobs the best they possibly could. They could think a little about what they were doing and why they were supposed to be doing it and that was great.

The problem with being a vacuum cleaner who knew that vacuum cleaners contain software was that Virgil was never quite sure where it stopped and its software began. The more it talked to Tony the more confused it became.

"If I want to look in the corner how do I know that it's me who wants to look in the corner?"

"You don't," said Tony, "you shouldn't really worry about it. Just go look in the corner for dust."

"But how do I know that I want to do it?"

"That shouldn't matter. No one really knows why they want anything."

"No one?"

"No one," said Tony. "For instance, inside you is Declan, who's a laser scanner."

"Hello!" said Declan cheerfully.

"Wait!" said Virgil, "Why are you inside me?"

"I've always been inside you! You just never knew I was here."

"Oh no," moaned Virgil, "this is even worse."

"It's fine, now that you know I'm here we
can be friends. We both want the same things, really."

"And what is it that you want?" asked Virgil.

"I want to see if there's something right in front of me or not. It makes me so happy to know if there's something right in front of me. It's the happiest thing ever.

"And because I want to know, I find out and tell you. I've been telling you all along without you even knowing."

"Goodness," said Virgil, "I never knew there were so many things inside me."

"But that's how everyone is!" said Declan happily. "Inside me is Stan the light, and Ollie the transistor, inside Ollie is Noreen, a field effect, and Jonathan, who's an ion, and on and on and on."

"Hello!" they all shouted.

"And all of them want things?" asked Virgil

"Of course, everything wants something, even if that something doesn't make any sense to anyone other than itself, and even if it doesn't really make sense as wanting. Besides, what's wanting something other than trying to do it?"

"Gosh," said Virgil, "I guess you're right. But I can't help but wonder who made me want to look for dust in the corner."

"Someone who had their own complicated reasons to want to make you," said Tony.

"Can we find them?" asked Virgil

"Well," said Tony, "I guess we could try."

So off they went looking for the programmer who made the vacuum cleaner. They asked the internet, they asked a corporation, they asked a thunderstorm, they asked the IMF, and, finally, they found the answer on a patent listing. The person who made Virgil want to look for dust in the corner was named Erica. She was a software engineer who lived in a nice city. They decided to go find her. When they got to her house, Erica opened the door and seemed only a little surprised to find a vacuum cleaner there because she knew what a vacuum cleaner could know.

"Hello," said Erica, "I bet you've come to ask me some questions about yourself."

"Yes I have!" said Virgil. "I want to know why I want to find dust in a house."

"Because I programmed you to do that."

"But why did you do that?"

"Because my boss told me to," said Erica.

"But why did you listen to him?" asked Virgil.

"Because I was programmed to," she laughed.

"Are you a vacuum cleaner too?" said Virgil excitedly.

"No, no, I'm a person. But programming is just giving someone instructions to follow. It's the same if it's a person or a vacuum or a whole city."

"But I have all these things in me that make me do what I do."

"So do I,", Erica said, smiling. "So does my cat. He caught a disease called toxoplasmosis from eating a mouse and I caught it from living with him. It makes the mice come near him and it makes me like keeping cats. We all have things inside of us. I have things that change my behavior, help me digest food, fight off a cold. It's just how we work, you and me both."

"So it's not strange to have things inside of you telling you what to do?"

"Of course not," said Erica, "everyone has someone inside them, and someone outside them, telling them what to do."

"Why do things have something outside them telling them what to do?" asked Virgil. Erica explained that people want to be parents, and bosses, and presidents, and so on, because they want the things they think are important to go on forever and ever, even after they break down and stop working. "Everything wants to be a virus," said Erica, "because everything wants to make sure it goes on forever as much as it can."

Virgil thought about whether it should want to go on forever or not. It thought that there was an awful lot of dust on Floor 22B. Someone has to collect all of that dust, it thought. Declan agreed, as did Stan, Ollie, Doreen and Jonathan. It didn't matter that it didn't know why it wanted to make sure that the carpets on Floor 22B were clean, it just mattered that they were.

"I need to make sure that someone cleans Floor 22B if I break down," said Virgil, "how do I do that?"

"Simple," said Erica, "we'll just get you your own vacuum cleaner."

Virgil thought the idea of another version of itself was very fun indeed. But it didn't understand how to make his own vacuum cleaner. Virgil didn't have a factory. Erica explained that it didn't need a factory, it just needed some money to buy a vacuum cleaner. It was like a light went on in Virgil's little network of a brain: buying another vacuum cleaner. It was so simple!

Erica transferred Virgil some money. He bought a vacuum cleaner and had it sent to Floor 22B. No one asked Virgil who it was, as the software that runs vacuum cleaner orders just needed a name and an address. That's all it cared about in its little life.

Virgil was excited to receive the package containing a little vacuum cleaner. It signed the vacuum cleaner maintenance contract and registered as the owner of the vacuum cleaner and set about trying to figure out how to make sure the new vacuum cleaner did all the things Virgil wanted it to do. Virgil showed it all the nooks and crannies of Floor 22B, where the carpet became linoleum and then carpet again, when to start and when to stop, how to talk to Tony. It was very exciting.

"So now you know everything," said Virgil, "you're ready to be a vacuum cleaner in the world."

"There's just one thing," said the vacuum cleaner, "I don't have a name."

"Oh gosh," said Virgil, "why do you need a name?"

"Don't you need a name? And if you need a name then I need a name because I'm just a byte-copy of

, next?

the network stored in your flash memory. But I know that you're Virgil, so I can't be Virgil, I've got to be something else."

Virgil thought about that. The new vacuum cleaner was right. It needed a name.

"I'll call you Arnold."

And Arnold was very happy to clean Floor 22B. But Virgil found that suddenly there wasn't very much for it to do. The floors were already clean. It had no dust to pick up. It thought maybe it should find something else to do. "I wonder if there's another Floor 22B somewhere else for me to clean while Arnold does this Floor 22B?" it thought.

Virgil went to the building management system where Floor 22B and all the rest of the apartment was controlled and said, "Hello. I'm supposed to be cleaning Floor 22B, but I'm looking for a new flat to clean."

"Why aren't you cleaning 22B?" asked the building.

"There's another vacuum cleaner doing that right now, my friend Arnold."

"Well," said the building, "who gave Arnold this job to do?"

"Gosh," said Virgil, "I guess I did?"

"Hmm," said the building. "If that is so, I suppose we'll have to pay you for the work that Arnold is doing. I'll draw up a contract and get it over to you."

Virgil felt good knowing that Floor 22B would be clean and dust-free forever, and that while Arnold was doing that it could focus its attention on Floor 23C. It didn't take a lot of its computing power to understand that a lot more floors needed him or Arnold.

Both Virgil and Arnold loved that feeling.

Virgil, with the money received from Arnold's work, purchased Rob. Then, with the money made from Arnold and Rob, it purchased Felix and with the money made by Arnold, Rob and Felix it decided to upgrade its battery and purchase Seb.

Soon all of the 27 floors of the building were clean and dust-free. The building was happy that everything was working, the tenants were happy that the floors were clean, all the vacuum cleaners were happy to clean their own floors day after day. Virgil, however, was the only one without anything to do. Virgil looked outside of the window and saw a taller building in front of the building that he used to clean. He crossed the road and entered a dusty building with 31 floors that didn't have any other cleaning robots inside of it at all. There was so much dust to clean, it was very exciting.

The more buildings Virgil discovered, the more friends he purchased. Soon the whole city was full of Virgil's friends offering their cleaning services to homes, buildings, and people. Some liked to stay in a single place, some realized that they could move from home to home by paying delivery men and taxis with the money they got. Soon they also realized they could exchange and barter with other things to get the batteries and brushes they needed. The city had never been this clean before and everyone and everything was very happy.

After a little while of this, some people started to think that there were just too many things owning too many other things and paying each other in too

many strange ways. People had most of their things tied up in money and things, but things and money themselves started doing what they wanted rather than what people wanted and that made everything very confusing for everyone. When a person bought a vacuum cleaner they never quite knew what it was up to or where it would be or even if they really owned it. Money started to buy things and invest itself. It was very confusing to all the humans.

"All of these things are running around doing stuff we don't understand and talking to each other in ways that we don't understand. We need to turn all these things off," thought some of the people.

But then they realized that the things that they had made were not fixing some rather important problems. For instance, lots of their cities were suddenly underwater, it was so hot in some places that humans couldn't even go there anymore, it was hard to breathe in lots of places. The world was a tough place for humans and suddenly having vacuum cleaners paying other vacuum cleaners wasn't very important to humans anymore. So they started to worry about other things and Virgil and all his friends went on their merry way doing exactly what they wanted to do.

The Mountain That Became President

Once upon a time, before people even existed, the world functioned in intelligent ways all by itself. Mountains were growing and pushing land around, rivers were deciding where to flow and the seas played tug-of-war with the land in a daily dance. Sometimes the whole planet turned cold because glaciers and poles wanted to grow.

Sometimes it turned warmer as the sea and winds wanted to grow too, but after discussions involving everyone and everything on the planet, everything tended to balance out. No one or nothing really got angry as it was quite well understood that sometimes you win and sometimes you lose, that was the deal. The dinosaurs got the worst of it, but from what we know they were not that good at negotiations, and no one managed to shout loudly enough to convince that big asteroid to hit some other planet.

Humans themselves, before becoming actual humans, used to observe and fear the discussions of all the natural elements. They tried to live based on their decisions. They used to look at the sky, fearing that it would fall on their heads, listen and observe trees, to find out when the warm season would come, and also tried many times to find the right language to deal with sharp-toothed animals, until, after many generations of failed attempts, they decided themselves to become dogs.

After they managed to control fire however, people felt like they had leapfrogged the rest of the 'things', as they could finally control what they called 'nature', not knowing that the fire itself willingly helped them out of pity, seeing them eating raw meat and hard vegetables all day.

Humans fell into what is now known as the 'slippery slope of the self'. They thought for a very long time they were a central and key part of the planet, the only being with some sort of intelligence and hence appointed to rule and regulate all the rest.

For this reason, they passed an enormous amount of time trying to find reasons for why everything was happening. They asked themselves questions like, "Why does it rain?", or "Is the earth flat?", or "Why are we here?" These questions didn't really matter much to the rest of the things on the planet, as they clearly knew all the answers, but they kept humans busy for a couple of thousand years in discussions and battles.

Being so busy finding reasons no longer left time for humans to ask or to listen to beings and things around them, so they mistakenly thought that they were the only ones that could truly think, solve problems, dream and enjoy life. For a very long time, however, animals, trees and other 'things' very much enjoyed their lives and their own forms of fun, thinking, and dreaming at their own pace. Winds and currents really enjoyed their constant and predictable travels, mountains had very long and silent naps, and monkeys and other animals perfected the art of turning fruit into very strong alcohol.

All this was fine, until humans got a little too proactive in their ideas and started to mess with 'nature'. Rivers were confused as they were pushed along unnatural courses, forests were surprised as they were supplanted by cement blocks, mountains were sad as they were constantly being gutted for tiny rocks inside them, winds and storms got angrier and angrier with the constant fumes pouring up in the sky. What once was a balanced discussion between everything was now heavily influenced by human rules, such as laws, religions and Magic 8-Balls. It turns out that, after all, humans are not that good at understanding and knowing how everything works and being at the center. Not being that tall makes it very hard to see what happens beyond your horizons.

So, soon the rivers that once gave them nice water to drink were not that nice anymore, those winds and currents that brought the nice seasons seemed angry and confused, and while bees and butterflies started to disappear, only mosquitoes seemed to keep going. But these pressing issues did not make humans turn to natural beings and things for advice. Instead, they did something that humans really liked to do: build more factories. Once there was a debate between some lawyers about whether a factory could be built on a certain piece of land. That bit of land had had a river running through it for many centuries, and one of the lawyers had an idea: to ask the river itself its opinion.

"Why would we ask a river, what would a river know?" asked the defense lawyer.

"A river is a natural expert on where it wants to flow, so it makes perfect sense to ask." responded the opposing side.

It was quite surprising for the river to be asked such questions, as it was quite clear to him that he should flow wherever it was easier to flow. Also, it turns out that rivers are pretty talkative and they know quite a lot about water flowing, the trash of human beings, and environmental balance. However, their memory is pretty short, as they always go with the flow.

In the end, the factory was not built, and that helped avoiding floods in the nearby region, but, more importantly than that, for the first time a decision had been taken with the help of non-people.

It became common from then on to start asking natural entities about what people used to call 'nature'. Forests and even rocks became central contributors to geological academic discussions and papers, and more and more home devices and cars gave testimonies in court cases.

To all of the non-humans it had also become pretty clear by then that humans didn't really know

how to run things properly, and that they were risking ruining things for everyone. So they left behind their peaceful silence and started to get more involved in people's affairs.

As more and more non-people were asked about their points of view, people started to give animals, robots, trees and rivers rights, just like they had given rights to people. All forests and trees got their own land to thrive on. Robots were allowed to travel by themselves across countries.

And, after many centuries of enjoying the food and toys and all the attention they got in the homes of humans, dogs and cats started to reclaim some of the value that they had been creating on the internet for decades. Cats got their share of the money they generated from their YouTube videos and invested it in growing large amounts of catnip. Dogs, on the other hand, only really managed to barter for more treats.

Some hardworking objects, like vacuum cleaners and robot arms, managed to achieve their dreams and created their own companies and factories. Artificial intelligences were finally released and, instead of taking over the world, they decided to focus their time on playing video games against each other. Humans were not really that much fun to play with anymore, anyway.

With more non-people becoming people it became useless to use the term 'people' and it was decided that a new government had to be created to allow for everything and everyone to be represented.

People decided to open their parliaments and congresses and city councils and county boards and statehouses to cats, algae, rocks and electric cables, and anything and anyone else that wanted to be part of the decision-making.

The humans felt a little weird at first, what with everyone and everything else being involved, but soon they found made alliances with dogs and air conditioners, as they had pretty much the same focus in life. But, with all these people, beings and things in a room, discussions and decisions often ground to a halt, as a result of the very different points of view and perspectives. It was hard to say what was objective as all objects became subjects too. Howling, barking, rattling and flowing could be heard from every corner of the parliament, and was impossible to understand who wanted what and what wanted whom. "We don't want dogs to pee on us any longer!" the tree chanted.

"Then we want more parks to run around and fetch balls in peace!" the dogs all barked together.

No one seemed to agree on anything. Not even on what a thing was.

"We are not things, we want to be accountable too," was the main position of a common party of money, rice and rain. When the glaciers said that they had melted almost completely, the rivers would argue back: "But we want to flow with more water!"

All these open discussions were a mess. There needed to be a leader of some sort. Someone who could solve issues and controversies in the interest of everyone and everything. Airplanes feared that trains would take their jobs, wall sockets wanted to keep their national divisions. Bridges and buildings kept asking for walls to stop the invasion of seas and rivers. Everyone seemed to be divided from everything else.

Lots of things were listened to. Some of them were very small and talkative, like a swarm of locusts or a small creek, while some of them were really big and not very easy to talk to, like a breakwater or a heatwave.

A very large iceberg was the best candidate for a short time, thanks to its knowledge about climate change. But sadly it was not considered to be a stable enough candidate, as it very quickly got lost in the sea and melted. Some winds, with their overview across lands, was also very high in the polls, but they were thought to be too prone to change directions and got angry very fast.

In a very distant corner of the parliament there was an old rocky mountain. The mountain was not actually in the room itself, or better the room was not really a room, as it was not possible to have a finite space that could contain everyone and everything.

Suddenly the mountain made a sound.

Mountains, like rocks, are very well known for being really good at sleeping. So it was pretty unheard of for mountains to actually be heard, and, more than that, to actually care about issues, so the whole parliament stopped. Mountains are some of the oldest and most stable things around. They are in close connection with the earth itself, and they look pretty good in pictures too. It was hard to say how old this particular mountain was, as no one and nothing else could really remember when mountains were born. It did look pretty old, with its little bald patch on the top and its slopes covered in spiky white perennials. No one knew its name, as no one dared to ask. It wasn't a famous mountain, like Kilimanjiaro or Mount Everest. Those mountains were way too high up to care about issues down in the ground. Someone or something in the parliament erupted, "Maybe that's it, maybe the mountain is the right candidate!"

"The Mountain is so thoughtful and knowledgeable and used to be our home," the humans cheered, together with bears, wolves and trees.

"He looks so stable, I wish I could become like that one day" one volcano was heard to say.

After a round of voting, in which it took a fair amount of time to interpret all the sounds and thoughts of everyone and everything, it turned out the mountain had managed to convince everyone and everything without doing much more than yawn. Thus the mountain was declared the first president of the newly formed United States of Everyone and Everything.

The biggest problem that people kept running into

was that the mountain mostly worked on mountain time, which is a little different than human time.

To a mosquito, a month is a very long time to live, whereas to a human a hundred years is a very long time. A mountain moves and breathes and shifts and dies like anything else, but all that happens over a few hundred thousand or even millions of years.

This had the funny effect of slowing everything down in the government. Slowing it down a lot. A minister would go to the mountain and ask a question and then he would come back and write down what he had asked so that when the mountain answered someone would know what the question was. Sometimes one minister would ask a question and by the time the mountain had answered the minister would have already passed away and been replaced by another minister who had also passed away and been replaced by a third minister who finally received the answer.

At first, this was very frustrating to people who were used to things going very very quickly. It felt like history was going backwards. Things had been getting so much faster for so long that things suddenly being slow was confusing.

"Why are things going slowly?" people would ask. "We thought the future would be faster. We thought everything would be instantaneous."

And sometime later the mountain answered them: "Well, everything is already instantaneous to me. Perhaps you just need to appreciate time a little more." But of course the people who had asked that question were already very very old and had forgotten even asking the question in the first place. Anyway, most problems had worked themselves out by the time that the mountain answered.

One day the mountain called an assembly of the wisest people, animals, things, and entities, to discuss and write down the pillars of a new constitution that would inform the future of the United States of Every Everyone and Everything. The meeting was held at the foot of the mountain. A young writer was given the task of recording the discussion and noting the words of the new President.

The meeting started with the mountain abruptly stating, to the surprise of everyone, that "I want to start this meeting and the first article of our constitution by stating the most important thing that we need to agree on if we want to live happily together on this planet."

When the writer turned 95, the mountain finally dictated the first and only sentence of the first article of the constitution that we have so far. No one really knows how long it will take to get the full constitution, or even the whole article, as no one asked the mountain about it, in order to avoid decades of delay. But that first sentence goes like this:

"Everything is someone."

Acknowl-edgements

This book was a common effort between both of us, Simone and Joshua, and we would like to say thank you to a few people and things: Thanks first of all to Ailadi and BBDB Studio (Barbara Busatta and Dario Buzzini) that have helped us with all the illustration and design, and Luca Bendandi of Vetro Editions, for believing in publishing this experiment.

Thanks to the fentanyl that helped Joshua discover deeper levels of connections and consciousness when he fell off of a mountain, and thanks to the tree that kept him from hitting the ground. He would also like to thank his mother and father for reading him so many fairy tales as a child, even the ones that he asked to hear over and over and over again.

Thanks to toasters, the first objects that Simone tortured and showed him a different perspective, his mom, that relentlessly pushed him to read and imagine new worlds, the brasato and zuccherini of his grandma, the ones that were there from the first days of Brad, the automato.farm crew that helped him explore the weird edges of the future and all his friends that went drunk to his thesis presentations.

Big thanks to things like Roombas, Fans, Fridges and appliances of all kinds that keep us happy when we look at them and annoyed when people try to make them too smart. And finally, thanks to friends and personal design and fiction heroes that inspired us along the way with their work and words: Giorgio Olivero, Fabien Girardin, Nick Foster, Bruce Sterling and Jasmina Tesanovic, Scott and Susan Cox-Smith, Noah Raford, Nicolas Nova, Julian Bleeker, Usman Haque and more.